parents

Translation: Jean Grasso Fitzpatrick

© Parramón Ediciones, S.A.
First Edition, April, 1985
The title of the Spanish edition is *los padres*

All inquiries should be addressed to:
Barron's Educational Series, Inc.
250 Wireless Boulevard
Hauppauge, New York 11788

Library of Congress Catalog Card No. 87-11398

International Standard Book No. 0-8120-3852-5

Library of Congress Cataloging-in-Publication Data

Solé Vendrell, Carme, 1944 –
   Parents.

   (The Family)
   Translation of: Los padres.
   Summary: Discusses briefly the role of parents in raising and
caring for children and how the feelings of the child can affect
those of the parents.
   1. Parents — Juvenile literature. [1. Parent and
child]   I. Parramón, José María. II. Title. III. Series.
Solé Vendrell, Carme, 1944 –   . Family.
HQ755.8.S6513   1987   306.8'74   87-11398
ISBN 0-8120-3852-5

Legal Deposit: CO-779-87

Printed in Spain by Graficromo
Polígono ''Las Quemadas''
Córboba (España)

7   8   9   9960   9   8   7   6   5   4   3   2   1

the family

parents

Carme Solé Vendrell

J. M. Parramón

BARRON'S

New York • Toronto • Sydney

This is how people become parents....
First they fall in love.

Then they get married.

Then they have a baby – you!

They feed you.

They dress you.

They bathe you.

They help you learn how to walk.

They help you learn how to play.

They teach you how to love.

And they bring you to school so you can learn

to read and write.

They feel sad when you're sick in bed.

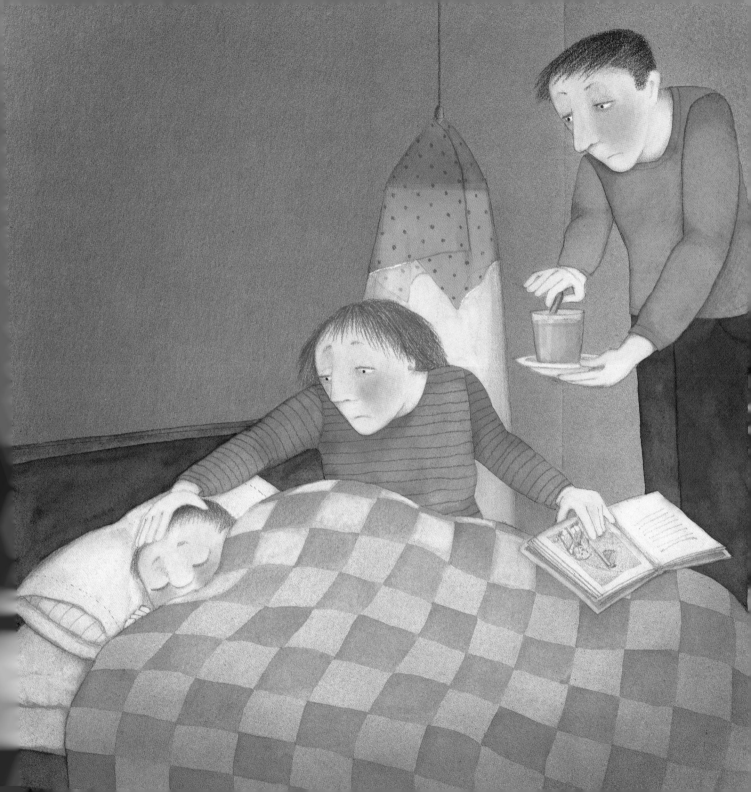

They're happy when you're running and jumping and laughing.

They're your parents!

PARENTS

Proud to be parents

The birth of a child is undoubtedly the most amazing moment in the life of a couple. But having a child also means accepting the responsibility to care for, feed and educate this new person. The process offers many satisfactions, no matter how many sacrifices and hours of worry.

"As the twig is bent"

The old saying is true — the home environment, and what parents do and say, have enormous influence on the way their child grows up. Although some aspects of the human personality are instinctive (survival, aggression, etc.), children's physical and mental development — and especially their ability to get along with people — depend in large part on the people closest to them, their parents.

The best gift

Spending our time and money teaching our children — to talk, dress themselves, eat, read and write, play sports, and study — is the best gift we can give. A Chinese folk tale makes the point very well: Once upon a time there was an old fisherman who went fishing with his son every day. The two knew all about fish, hooks, and bait. One day, the son asked the father, "Father, can I catch a fish to give to a friend of mine who is hungry?" The father agreed. The next day, the son asked the father for another fish: "Father, my friend was very happy yesterday, because he and his brother had food to eat. Can I catch another fish for him?" And then the father replied, "Yes, my son. But you would be doing your friend a bigger favor if instead of giving him a fish every day, you would teach him how to fish."

What can parents do?

Day by day children continue to grow, maturing in body and developing in personality. And all the while they are making new friends, studying, and working toward their independence.

What can parents do during this difficult process? First of all, they can continue to set a good example by being loving, honest, and fair. After all, they have always shown their love by teaching their child right from wrong, helping with schoolwork, and keeping in touch with teachers. And by continuing to be understanding, trying to remember how they themselves were as youngsters, and by remembering that times have changed, chances are they will be happily surprised at how their children grow toward independence.

Adulthood begins around the age of twenty. In general, couples get married between the ages of twenty and thirty.